NATIONAL GEOGRAPHIC

My Bean Plant

T0052107

Joseph Cicianc

I can grow a bean plant.
This is what I need:

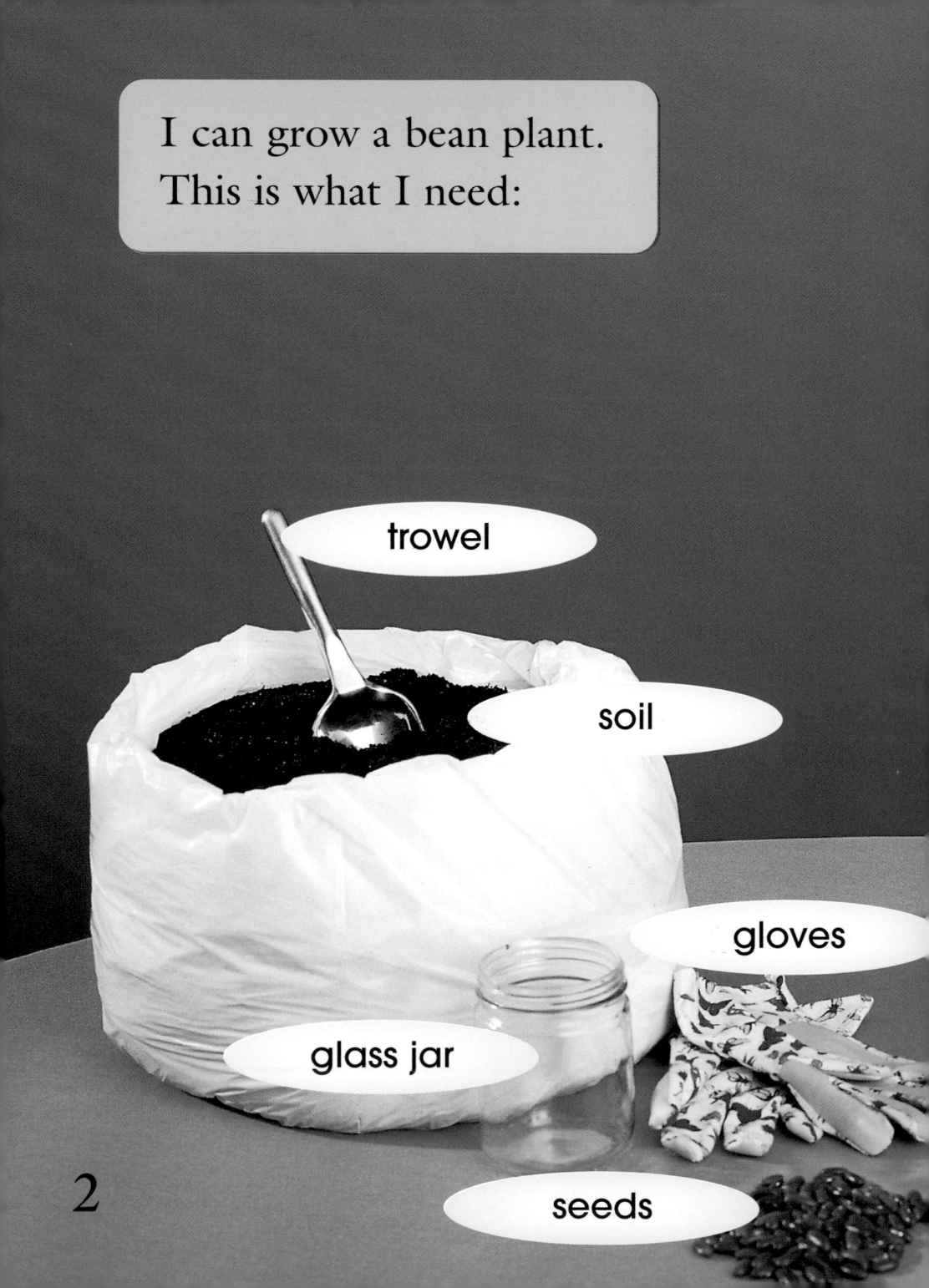

flower pot
watering can
paper towels

First, I fold the paper towel and put it in the jar.

Next, I fill the jar with water.
Then, I put the seeds inside the jar.

I check on the seeds.
They are starting to grow.

I can see a root growing from the bottom of a seed.
I can see a shoot growing from the top of a seed.

My bean plant is growing bigger.
I can see the roots growing from
the bottom of the plant.

I can see the long stem.
I can see the leaves.

I put my bean plant into a pot.

I water my bean plant.
Little white flowers are growing on
my bean plant.

Bean pods are growing on my bean plant.

Some of the bean pods are ready to be picked.

What's inside the pods?
Beans!
beans

Picture Glossary

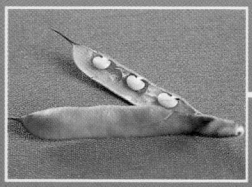

beans

roots

flower

seeds

leaves

shoot

pod

stem